BRILLIANT U

19 Inspirational Tips
For Creating The Life You Want

By Star Zuwala, MA

Edited by Nina Cherry

Balboa Press books may be ordered through booksellers or by contacting:

Balboa Press
A Division of Hay House
1663 Liberty Drive
Bloomington, IN 47403
www.balboapress.com
844-682-1282

Because of the dynamic nature of the Internet, any web addresses or links contained in this book may have changed since publication and may no longer be valid. The views expressed in this work are solely those of the author and do not necessarily reflect the views of the publisher, and the publisher hereby disclaims any responsibility for them.

Any people depicted in stock imagery provided by Getty Images are models, and such images are being used for illustrative purposes only. Certain stock imagery © Getty Images.

ISBN: 978-1-9822-6780-3 (sc)
ISBN: 978-1-9822-6781-0 (e)

Library of Congress Control Number: 2021908171

Print information available on the last page.

Balboa Press rev. date: 07/12/2021

BALBOA.PRESS
A DIVISION OF HAY HOUSE

DEDICATION

To my husband, Steve, thank you from the bottom of my heart. Your consistency, reliability, total commitment, love, kindness, and humor was exactly what I needed in order to bring my heart fully back to life. I am forever grateful that you helped me find my faith in God and that we created a happy family together. We are super fortunate to have found the love that we have!

To my daughter, Lexy, being your mother has been one of the greatest things to happen to me. Since the day you were born my heart has felt such intense and beautiful feelings of love and joy. You are a bundle of pizzazz and you always remind me of the importance of having fun. We are blessed to have each other!

To my mother, Nina, thanks for always believing in me, supporting me and encouraging me to be who I am in full force.

To my family, friends and everyone else who has been kind and loving to me. It has been highly appreciated! You helped keep my fire stay lit.

INTRO

First and foremost, this book is for anyone who is wanting to tap into the knowledge of how to create an awesome and beautiful life that they envision for themselves. They are willing to put forth the necessary effort at improving, developing and possibly healing themselves to make room for a greater capacity for success, happiness and contentment.

I am proud to say that I am a success story of overcoming huge obstacles and working at making my life a success! I know that you can too. Happiness, contentment, satisfaction, and success is mine. I know that it can be yours too! It was not easy at times to keep on the path and I doubted if it would ever happen for me. But I knew what I wanted and I went after it with intense determination, no matter what others said or did to try and stop me. Making it out of the darkness and into the light is one of the greatest accomplishments of my life. Happiness and having inner peace is true massive wealth! I know many people who have money, friends, and look like they have it all from the outside view. But in reality, they are really struggling and suffering on the inside. Truly having it all inside and out is the bomb. And everyone wants it! Some have it. Some of those who have it teach others how to have it all too! That is all heart! Helping others is such a great service to the world.

Making it to the mountain top myself, I decided I wanted to help others get to there as well. So, I started writing how I went about doing it. I wanted to uplift and inspire others and fill them with the hope that creating the life that they have always wanted for themselves is possible. Having a beautiful life can be a reality! This book is for people who might feel that they are in the darkness and are searching for the light or searching for the way to make positive, long lasting changes. This book is full of suggestions on how to reach the mountaintop of success.

Writing this book is a way to share the knowledge that I have passionately and tirelessly worked at acquiring for over 25 years. Those years include a Bachelor's Degree in Theatre, a Master's Degree in Marriage and Family Therapy, and countless hours of research on many different subject matters. One of the areas I focused primarily on was healing from trauma and abuse.

I found that the point of power is at the source of how one feels. If you feel fabulous, you easily go forth with the fiery energy fueling it all. You have longevity and fixed power that does not wane. To be fully connected to the self is to be at the controls of the rocket blasting off! Connecting with the power source comes when the emotions are heard and honored.

Another important ingredient in achieving goals is having a map to help you get to the destination. The map must be credible. It must be given to you by someone who has made the journey successfully. The map should have clear goals with an action plan with concrete steps to reach the goals.

I know that change is possible because I have seen it in my own life and in the lives of countless clients I have worked with. The progress that was seen and experienced was in feeling better, making better decisions, an increase in positive thinking, living with greater contentment and more worldly success. Where there was a question mark of doubt there now is an exclamation point of assurance. I do give credit to God, as He has been one of the constant lights in my life, leading me to creating a brilliant life.

Success can happen when a person takes the responsibility of creating the sunshine in their own life, rather than waiting for it to happen to them. They take a proactive position. Basically, they do the work! They start seeing the results. Keep in mind, practice makes it permanent. So, keep at it until it comes to fruition.

These tips are only suggestions. They will give you food for thought.

TESTIMONIAL

There was a time in my life when I was living with an abusive boyfriend. I was blind to much of the abuse I was receiving. Star woke me up.

Currently, my life has taken an amazing turn recently, and I have the wisdom of the ages, passed on through Star, to thank for my readjusted vision for myself. Her sharp intelligence and a knack for creative thinking and problem solving have taken me through many, many troubled times. With a compassion that knows no bounds and a quick, wicked wit, Star has helped me rebuild myself into someone I can be proud of. Most importantly I think, she has always urged me to put myself first, and to take care of the wounds that reappear until they are completely healed. This healing work is done best by those who, like Star, have a deep well of knowledge, experience, creativity, and love. I will always be her #1 fan!

-S. M.

CONTENTS

BE DETERMINED – IT'S THE KEY TO SUCCESS

Goal: Achieve What You Want

Wouldn't it be amazing to know that you can have what you want? Your vision of getting more inner peace, contentment, positivity, success and overall wellbeing is possible and could bring you greater happiness in your personal and professional life as well. There are many different steps that go into achieving these great goals.

You must see yourself as a visionary and builder. It starts with an idea or vision, then plans are made, then the process starts of implementing the plans. The process takes as much time as it takes, and each part that is built is an essential part of the whole. Trust the process!

Perseverance is an essential part in the achievement of goals. You must also believe in yourself, in your current skills and your ability to develop new skills. It is good to recognize the progress made even if it is small. Be ok with failure. Be ok with not being perfect. Be kind with yourself along the way when you might fall down and stumble in your obtaining of knowledge. The more beneficial information you bring in, the more you will get a solid footing and then you will get better and better and better!

Achieving what you want, requires work! Hard work and a lot of effort. It requires feeding the fire inside you. When you feel good and are filled with passion for what you want, it will help you connect with the energy needed to make it happen! Keep your eye on the prize!

If you don't have anyone for support or encouragement, post inspiring and uplifting notes for yourself on a mirror that give you the support you need. If it doesn't exist, create it! You can be your own support! You know what you need better than anyone! These notes are important because they will help you to keep going in those times that you may want to give up!

Action Plan:

1. **Make a list of what you want to achieve**
2. **Research it. Educate yourself fully by reading everything about it**
3. **Get yourself fired up! Learn how to be a morale booster**
4. **Do it. Work it. Practice it every day**
5. **The more you practice, the better you will get**

SUCCESS SAYING - "I CAN do this! I believe in myself! I can keep going!"

BE GRATEFUL DAILY

Goal: Create Abundance

Being appreciative for what you already have in your life breeds a grateful heart and creates the capacity for even more abundance to be attracted into your life. It starts by taking stock of what you have. Make a list. It can sometimes be only one thing on the list that you can think of. One thing is more than none. Life is a lot about how we look at it!

Some suggestions to put on the list are simple things like being healthy and feeling good. Those are huge blessings. When you are healthy and feeling good, you wake up every morning and meet the day with pizzazz! You wake up hopeful and motivated and inspired. It is as if a fire is lit. Lighting the fire within is a significant part of the equation to achieving what you want! I will share with you a powerful secret. Here it goes. What you think affects how you feel and then ultimately what you do. There is tremendous power in that sentence. It is a potent and real way of looking at your life. If your thoughts are positive, then your self-talk will be positive and with that powerful force, your actions will be as well. Be careful what you think; if your thoughts are negative, you can put the fire out as well. Be sure to think in terms of abundance and fortune! There are unlimited things to be grateful for if you look for them! The key is to train your brain to look for them!

The beauty in doing this, is that the more you think of things that brighten your outlook, the more you will be filled with a feeling of peace and contentment. By focusing on and appreciating what you do have, the more the dissatisfaction and frustration dissipates, and it is replaced by upliftment and fulfillment.

Action Plan:

1. **Wake up every day and make a list of the blessings in your life**
2. **Make a list of what you appreciate about yourself**
3. **Find the positive in every situation**
4. **Strive for balance in appreciating what you have and also putting energy into going after what you want**

SUCCESS SAYING - "I always see the many the blessings in my life!"

BRING FORTH THE SUNSHINE

Goal: Turning Your Inner Light On

You create your reality by the thoughts that you think the decisions that you make and by what you do. But, something that a lot of people don't know, is that you create more effectively when all the parts of you are utilized. What I mean by that, is when you acknowledge, honor, nurture, and listen to your emotional nature you can harness that power in your quest for solid gains. Say you want to create a wonderful and bright reality for yourself. That which you focus on is what you create. Thoughts have life and they affect the emotional self. Thoughts are seeds that you plant and how you nurture them is how they grow. Every time that you think a certain thought, it is as if you are nurturing your emotional self which is symbolically watering the seeds and making them grow. Be mindful of what you are thinking and how it is affecting how you feel. It can greatly influence your desired creation.

Have you ever noticed people who are happy and wonder how they can be so full of life and joy and confidence? They could have been born into a family that encouraged them. Good for them! The truth is, a lot of people were not so lucky, but don't get discouraged. It can still be within your reach. It can be yours! It takes daily practices of encouraging, supportive and loving thoughts which make you feel great! Champions and winners know they have to hype themselves up, cheerlead for themselves and pump up their good vibes to a high frequency. They are feeding and nurturing the emotional self! That power is tremendous and marvelous to reign in and utilize! That is the same for anyone else who is going after their dreams.

Basically, it is learning how to build your confidence. Nurturing, controlling and mastering the inner fire and knowing it is an essential part in helping you build the empire you desire. See it, be it, and own it! Start creating an environment which is positive and feels good, feels great and then becomes completely fabulous! It is a progression. Learn how to feed the momentum until it gets stronger and stronger!

The other part of the equation is being around people who are supportive, kind, caring, encouraging, trustworthy, and in your corner. Seek to align with people who are similar to who you are and also are who you want to be! Choose to limit your time or remove yourself from negative or hurtful people. Do things that make you happy, healthy and radiant. For example, playing your favorite music, rollerblading, biking, walking, hiking, painting, craft making, decorating, dancing, photography, cooking, writing, watching the ocean, or sitting in the sunshine. Doing what you love helps you find the inner light. Connect with your heart and you will always win! Learn how to bring the party vibe, instead of waiting for it to come to you.

Action Plan:

1. **Be aware of your what you do – Does it make you feel good or bad?**
2. **Influence your day by doing what makes you feel fabulous**
3. **Incorporate new healthy activities to turn the inner light on**

SUCCESS SAYING - "This moment is bright & full of wonderful possibilities."

BE IN THE DRIVER'S SEAT OF YOUR LIFE

Goal: In Charge Of Yourself And Your Life

Are you in the driver's seat or the passenger's seat of your life? The seat you are in determines where you will go in life. Your choices make your life what it is. Are you over the age of 18 and an adult? You can take responsibility and take charge of your life. What that means is to strive for independence and kick dependence to the curb. Kick any victimization and helplessness to the curb. Be a doer who figures out solutions to any problems. Make blaming and complaining a thing of the past. Say, "I can do it! I will do whatever it takes to seek out answers and figure it out! There is a way. I can also pray for answers to come!"

Here are more ways of implementing an "I can" way of thinking: say to yourself every day, "I believe in myself. I can help myself. I don't need anyone else to do things for me that I can do for myself. I am an adult and am responsible for taking care of myself financially, emotionally, mentally, physically and spiritually." It is about empowering yourself. Ask yourself, would the particular thought or action I am considering, fit with the person I would most admire? Look at the possible consequences of those actions and what they could be. Also, know that if you head in a direction that is not where you want to be going, you can make different choices NOW!

Focusing on self-improvement is like announcing that you know that you are worth it and the investment is a good one. Working towards improving is a beneficial way to spend your time. Take care of yourself by giving yourself what you need in order to be happy- like safety, true regard, self-care, loving thoughts and actions, comfort, excitement and adventure. That is how you become independent and in charge of your life. You don't wait for others to be it or do it for you!

Action Plan:

1. **Choose to take on responsibility rather than avoid it**
2. **Adopt a "I can figure it out" stance and seek answers**
3. **Take care of yourself emotionally, know what you need to be happy**

SUCCESS SAYING - " I enjoy taking on responsibility. I am capable."

BRILLIANT U TIP #5

BUILD YOUR DESIRED SELF

Goal : Become The Person You Admire Most

You have to take action to develop yourself into who you want to be. Who do you respect and why? What makes them an incredible or awe-inspiring person? Learn how to integrate those qualities into your life. Everyone has the capability to connect with their personal power and make things happen! Tapping into the "how" is the key. Remarkable people seem to have similar qualities. Here is a list and a tip on how to develop each quality:

Graceful in stressful situations- Is direct but kind and fair to all.

Unforgettable huge heart– Thinks of and does things for others (in balance).

Confident- Knows their value and what they have to offer the world.

High self-esteem- Won't allow others to mistreat them. Demands to be treated with respect. Walks away from the relationship, if need be.

Is fearless (safely)- Is a trendsetter and takes risks that are thought out.

Knows their strengths – Focuses on things that they are good at. Accepts or works on their weaknesses (if possible).

Surpasses expectations- Is driven to be the best that they can be.

Vital and bright- Is Full of life and passion for their interests.

Independent- Is Self-sufficient. Strong sense of who they are and what is right for them, separate from anyone else.

Solution oriented- Knows there are always solutions and goes about finding them. Tries to refrain from complaining or blaming.

Is grateful & humble- Thanks God or their higher power for every blessing in their life. Knows their blessings are on loan from God or the higher power.

Radiant- Is connected to their inner fire, passion and heart.

Action Plan:

1. **Make a list of qualities of the people you respect and admire most**
2. **Research the qualities in depth and how they are put into play**
3. **Put them into play by practicing them daily**

SUCCESS SAYING - "I have the courage to improve myself.
I know that I can be the person I want to be."

BRILLIANT U TIP #6

BE A WINNER. KNOW YOUR WORTH.

Goal: High Self-Esteem

Having a winner's mentality aka high self-esteem is vital to a brilliant life. When you were a child, people around you influenced how you valued yourself and how you saw youself through the experiences you had with your family members, friends of the family, playmates and schoolmates. Like a sponge, you might have picked up information of who you were and your value by how you were treated. How you are treated can affect your self-esteem greatly. When you turn 18 and become an adult, you can then choose who to keep close to you, what experiences to allow into your life, and what to limit or walk away from. All of these new choices affect your self-esteem as well.

You can shed any feelings of helplessness or beliefs that you are trapped by your past or thoughts that you are unworthy of good things. If others have treated you badly (or treat you badly now) it has nothing to do with your innate value. It is only information. You can have high self-esteem again regardless of what others do or don't do. It can be healed and built up again. Listen to your inner dialogue of what you think of yourself. Tune into the part of you that knows who you are and your value, separate from anyone else's opinion of you. Independent thought is a huge gift you can give yourself. You are valuable. You are important. You are talented in someone way, you just have to discover in what way that is!

Knowing yourself is tapping into a power some will never experience. To be in your power is to be at the source of creation, and that has impact on everything around you, and your future, too.

A winner has high self-esteem, a strong sense of self, total belief in themselves, can assure themselves and is connected to their fire!

Action Plan:

1. **Build a high self-esteem with loving thoughts**
2. **It starts with you knowing that you are worthy of good things**
3. **Adopt a winner's mentality of finding solutions to every problem**
4. **Seek to align with people who are dynamic, non-judgmental, celebratory, and open-minded**
5. **Be in your heart and you will always win!**

SUCCESS SAYING - " I know who I am and I am of value!"

BE UNAFRAID TO ASK FOR WHAT YOU NEED AND WANT

Goal: Know What You Need. Not Settling For Less.

Being fearless in asking for what you need and want in life is critical in order to get what you want. If you never ask, you will never get it. Be honest with yourself about what you need and what you want. Self-reflect. Honor your emotions. Your heart and emotions will tell you what you need from life and from another in order to be happy in a relationship. Know your deal breakers. Be ok with the reality that people can choose to tell you no, as it will be dependent on what they want for their lives. If you honor, love yourself and want the best for you, you will be ok with their response. It is only information that is being relayed to you. The other person has an opportunity to meet your needs or give you what you want (within reason). If they don't want the same things as you, you have an opportunity to then choose what is right for you or where you want to go from that point.

Some of the most important needs in life:
To love and be loved/ To be important to another
To be accepted/ To trust/ To feel safe
To have good health/To be content/To be at home in your body

Everyone has the free will to make the choice of what they want to do. Make sure that you are on the same page with another person and that you want the same things. This will maximize the harmony in your life and relationships. This is your life. Make your happiness now. Make smart decisions about who you get involved with because that choice will affect your life significantly. Getting what you need emotionally from someone who wants the same things are you do is vital, yet remember it needs to come from yourself too! Give yourself what you need so that you are not dependent upon another.

Action Plan:

1. **Get clear on what you need in intimate relationships and friendships**
2. **Ask for what you need and want**
3. **Be ok with another's answer – Know what you want and do what is right for you**
4. **Be ok on your own**
5. **Be strong enough to be alone when need be**

   SUCCESS SAYING - " I will ask for what I want and need, that which is best for me."

HAVE MOXIE! REACH FOR THE STARS!

Goal: Be A Go Getter

You know those people who are bright, shiny and confident. You can feel it when they enter the room. They have presence. They know what they want and they just go after it with the expectation that it is theirs. They command respect because they know themselves fully. They own their power and use it to their advantage. Some are born with it and some build that in themselves by emulating qualities. The go getter quality is one that is truly admirable! It is action incarnate. Initiators and they don't wait for other's permission. They just do it! They have accessed the gold mine of their powerful forceful nature and manifestation flows from them like liquid gold. It is truly awesome to behold.

You have to be daring in life to dream big and you must fiercely protect your dreams along the way while you work at them. Dreams give you direction, meaning to your life, as well as purpose and passion. In order to make dreams real, you have to connect with your passions! Passion is an unmatched motivating force that is always available to tap into to! The beauty is, no one can ever take it from you! Connecting with what you love is the starting point of the journey. One way to connect and see your passion is to create a collage to help you envision it and allow it motivate you while you work at making it real! A vision board can be a very powerful tool and worthwhile project to help you to define and ground your ideas. Writing ideas down, as well as creating vision boards can help with the manifestation process. You have to see it. You have to live it. you have to own it! Then embody it! You have to make it real!

Define what you love. What are your dreams?

Doing photography	**Climbing a mountain**
Creating art	**Finding love**
Modeling	**Being happy / Being Content**
Acting/ Singing	**Having a career**
Having inner peace and tranquility.	**Learning a trade**
Being a musician or composer	**Being at home in one's own body**
Playing an instrument	**Getting healthy/ Getting in shape**

Action Plan:

1. **Develop your courage by being unafraid of the unknown**
2. **Being ok with not being perfect in order to begin**
3. **Loving yourself totally. Being ok with failure. Seeing it as a necessary part of building what you want**

SUCCESS SAYING -" I have the courage to try out different things!"

TAKE STOCK OF YOUR THOUGHTS

Goal: Reprogramming & Controlling The Mind

Taking stock of your thoughts and what you are thinking is one of the first steps to changing outdated ways of being such as changing a doubtful outlook to one that is sure and excited. Becoming aware of the exact thoughts you think, writing them down and coming up with alternate empowered possibilities is the way to start reprogramming the mind to work for your best outcome. Focus on "practice makes excellence". No matter if you catch your thoughts being negative, you can always rewrite and replace! Changing your attitude can be a reality, because negativity is never permanent. Intention is another powerful tool to utilize. Work it and keep working it until it is here and natural.

Re-programming the mind takes time, so be patient while being mindful. Encourage yourself while becoming free of doubt, anxiety or fear. This change occurs through repetitious positive thoughts and loving actions towards yourself at every moment. And lots of them! The reason why it takes lots of positive experiences is that you need to reassure yourself that positivity is real. It is almost like your mind doesn't believe that it can be real, especially if you have had a past of many negative experiences.

During the process, you may notice that you fall back into a negative way of thinking. That is ok. Try have compassion for yourself. Negative thinking can be a sign that there is just more of a need for conscious positive correction. The point of power is now! A way to re-train the brain is to read inspiring phrases, watch uplifting programs, and be around encouraging and kind people. You are basically rewiring the brain! It is bringing new experiences into the equation to carve new neurological pathways of being. This new you and this new life is going to be everything that you dreamed it to be! By bringing in these new great experiences in abundance that make you happy, you will look forward to more and look backwards less and less. Onward and upward to great things!

Action Plan:

1. **Assess your thoughts where you have doubts and fears**
2. **Write the fears and doubts down**
3. **Write alternative positive thoughts for each doubtful thought**
4. **Create a mantra of these positive thoughts**
5. **Say these positive mantras as many times as needed**
6. **Get excited about what you want and where you want to go!**

SUCCESS SAYING - " I am focused on becoming more positive in my thoughts."

BE OPENMINDED!

Goal: Open To All Avenues Of Information

There is so much information out there about how to make permanent change happen, if you are open to letting it come to you through the many different forms. You could be watching a movie and see a scene that moves you or gives you a great idea. You could open a book to a page on the exact issue that you have been trying to figure out. You can be talking to someone and they say exactly what you needed to hear for a major realization or breakthrough. You can be listening to a song and the words make something click in your understanding of a new way of looking at a situation. Kind of like magic! I call that God's or our higher power's awesome presence in our lives again leading us to what is best for us!

You must not stop in the quest for seeking the information. It is out there. Research! Research! Research! The more you seek, the more you will know and YES, KNOWLEDGE IS POWER! It is almost like the more you learn, the more you have access to greater parts of your brain that might have been elusive to you before now. Miracles do happen, and they happen more often to those who believe that they are possible.

Other great sources for critical information for healing and change are counselors, therapists, psychiatrists, medical doctors, priests, spiritual leaders and other professionals. Their knowledge can have a tremendous transformational impact on you and your life. There are many ways to the same destination. You can take what works for you! Only you know what is right for you! These professionals can help impart information that worked for them or that they have obtained for your benefit.

Open the door and let the information in! You are awakening the powerhouse in you and awakening parts of your mind to fully actualize yourself! Yay! It is happening! You are on your way!

Action Plan:

1. **Open your mind to allow the information in**
2. **Sift through all the information and take what works for you**
3. **What stands out to you and why?**
4. **Practice these new ideas or ways of being. Implement! Implement! Implement!**

SUCCESS SAYING –" I am open to information where ever it comes from."

TRUST YOURSELF

Goal: Trust Your Intuition

If you listen to your intuition you are blessed with the ability to close your eyes and connect with yourself in a deep and real way without anyone else's input. Your intuition can sometimes tell you everything that you need to know. How you feel about something can tell you to go forward, to stop, to wait, to take stock and to reflect. It might take practice to listen to your intuition and trust yourself. It takes honoring the emotions you feel and making space for them. Not being embarrassed by them or showing them. Have you ever wondered why people say, "Sorry, I am a mess right now," when they cry in front of others? It tells you something about that person's level of comfort with emotions.

Emotions are beautiful and informative. They need to be listened to. Grief, disappointments, hurts, embarrassments, frustrations, etc. are a part of life. Feeling those emotions and letting them go makes space for the greater capacity of positive emotions to take its place. See them as your greatest friend, take care of them, and listen to them! Sometimes difficult emotions can become overwhelming if you stay in the pain too long. Seek professional assistance if the need for help is immediate.

When you create a welcoming environment for emotions to communicate clearly to you, it assists you in being an independent thinker force and being forcefully proactive. It can also be a tool to help keep you safe. Dealing with people can be confusing sometimes. Dysfunctional people can lie, manipulate and use lower vibration ways of being, due to their inability to be real and communicate directly. If someone tells you one thing while the truth of the situation is quite different, it can be negatively overwhelming. But when you trust your intuition fully, it will tell you something is not right. You will feel it. That ability is a super power. And it is awesome!

Action Plan:

1. **Practice being comfortable with your own emotions and other's emotions**
2. **See emotions as wanting to communicate important information**
3. **See emotions as protective and as a friend**
4. **Trust the feelings that come up**
5. **Trust yourself**

SUCCESS SAYING - " Emotions are amazing. They are my ally, and I trust them."

BRILLIANT U TIP #12

HAVE THE STRENGTH TO ACCEPT LIFE AS IT IS

Goal: Graceful Acceptance

You cannot control some situations as they come up in your life. None the less, they will affect you. Having no control over things that happen to you can be very distressing. In order to keep one's calm and sanity, acceptance is the key. Keep in mind I am talking about situations that are stressful and distressing but not of the chronic violent, traumatic and abusive kind. No one should accept or allow those types of experiences. I am talking about the acceptance of the past and how it can help you to release built up anxiety and stress that can disrupt your inner peace. Leaning on God (or your higher power) to help you though the difficulty and being thankful for the help will allow miracles to happen to get you through. Grace is an important quality to develop in the face of life's non-violent challenging times. Life's challenges are a test of your ability to show your level of faith that all will work itself out and help will be there to assist you.

Giving up control is sometimes very hard to do, but doing so helps your psyche regain equilibrium and peace. Your peace of mind is priceless when in these disturbing situations. There will be those times where you cannot change another person and what they do or don't do. Know there is always something you can do about your side of the situation, even if it is to shift your own attitude.

Life is not all butterflies and sunshine. There are times of difficulty that we must get through or cope with reality as it is. Have faith that God will assist you in overcoming a sometimes-impossible situation.

Sometimes you need to breathe, step away, or go scream in the car or a private place is needed. Releasing the built-up emotions is for your own health! Life can be so difficult at times and there is so much uncertainty and unpredictability on a daily basis, so it is fabulous that you always have something to lean on that will helps you get through.

Action Plan:

1. **Assess each situation- Is it in your control or not?**
2. **Safety check. Am I safe? If not, seek help**
3. **If safe, breathe. Accept the past or the non-violent/traumatic present**
4. **Release pent up emotions**
5. **Thank your (or higher power) for bringing answers and being there for you**

SUCCESS SAYING – " I am at peace and I have faith that help is on the way."

GIVE YOURSELF THE BEST

Goal: Self- Care As A Priority

Be honest with yourself. Do you consider yourself worth care and good things? Are you worth protecting? Are you valuable? Your level of self-regard directly impacts what you think you deserve. Your outlook in life is a reflection of how valuable you are in your own mind. This is not about ego. This is about taking care of your needs on a daily, moment to moment basis. This is very important for those who have been mistreated because it can have an impact on your ability for self-care. There is always something that you can do to take care and re-charge your battery.

When you do self-care practices you show your level of regard for yourself! You help yourself to operate on the most optimum level you can! Make sure you are taking care of your needs in a holistic manner, which includes all levels: emotionally, spiritually, physically and mentally. All are vitally important for total brilliance!

Some examples:

- **Eat foods that are good for you**
- **Drink water every day**
- **Sleep/Rest/Time out away from stress**
- **Hot bath or shower**
- **Listen to music that uplifts and also relaxes**
- **Outdoor Activities- rollerblading, biking, hiking, etc.**
- **Indoor exercise- yoga, stretching, treadmill walking, etc.**
- **Beautifying & inspiring your environment**
- **Yard work/Gardening/ Sitting in the sun**
- **Pampering – face spritzer, lotions, foot creams**
- **Reading a novel or self-help book**
- **Writing in a journal**
- **Doing activities that bring you joy**
- **Talking to a friend or family member or someone you trust**
- **Use essential oils under your nose or in a diffuser**
- **Think thoughts and read material that make you feel good**
- **Treat yourself the way you always wanted to be treated**
- **Watch comedies and bring more laughter into your life**
- **Other:**_____

Action Plan:

1. **Assess your level of self-care and what is needed**
2. **Make a list of self-care practices**
3. **Start doing them daily**
4. **You can always add to the list**
5. **Congratulate yourself on taking greater care of yourself**

SUCCESS SAYING -"I am worthy of good things and I will give them to myself."

FORGIVE AND BE COMPASSIONATE

Goal: Emotional Freedom And Happiness

To be at our most effective and powerful, you have to release any emotional baggage that may be keeping you back or down. Sometimes that is due to having negative experiences with others. It is not easy to forgive others who have disappointed you, let you down or hurt you. You can help yourself let go of the baggage, by doing your part in forgiving them, by having compassion for them. They might be people who have been damaged by life and who might not have the capacity to care much about others. They might have been born without the capacity to care about others. People are known to make mistakes. That does not mean that you have to have them in your life, especially if they continue to hurt you. After the age of 18, you are technically an adult and you can decide who we want around you and who you don't. Ask yourself, "Do they treat me the way I want to be treated? Are they even capable of treating me good?"

You might find yourself reverting to feelings of being upset with someone who has hurt you. Staying in that negative place can get in the way of achieving what you want in life. What you focus on is what you get more of. Positivity breeds more positivity! Do yourself a solid and find the way to have compassion for people and forgive them, not for them, but for your emotional health and capacity for more abundance and joy.

If you are having a difficult time with this and need more assistance, contact a professional local counselor or therapist who specializes in your area of need. Feel good about it. You are doing everything you can to improve yourself and be the best you can! That is awesome and don't let anyone make you feel bad about it! You are here to do whatever it takes to achieve our dreams. Don't let anyone's small ways of thinking prevent you from attaining your dreams!

Action Plan:

1. **Assess who you may have difficulty forgiving or having compassion for**
2. **See them as human, not perfect and maybe damaged**
3. **Learn to forgive and release anger for your own emotional happiness**
4. **Love from afar if that is what is safest or best for you**

SUCCESS SAYING - "I choose what is best for me! I have compassion for others."

BRILLIANT U TIP #15

LIVE IN YOUR HEART

Goal: Love Unconditionally

Connecting with your heart more fully can be one of the greatest things that you can do! Self-acceptance and accepting others are well worth all the effort it can take. It happens when you give up the idea of perfection and replace it with being the best that you can be. Being a work in progress is completely ok too! You are ok as you are, yet you are striving to grow and improve. When you strive towards excellence rather than perfection, you are giving yourself a real chance at success. Perfection is impossible. Since it does not exist, it can stop all forward progress because you have failed before you even have begun. It is a good idea to refrain from expecting others to be perfect as it can lead to disappointment. Staying away from negativity is the key! Negativity can shut down the heart from loving.

When you learn to accept yourself and then love yourself just the way you are, you give yourself a huge present of unconditional love. You don't have to do anything to be loveable. You just are and that feels so good. In doing that, it can help you to love and have compassion for others. This is a powerful gift to give others as well. It can make you someone who comforts, warms, enlightens, and uplifts. To be around a kind and loving person who is non-judgmental and does not criticize you harshly is such a safe feeling. It is like the sun came out and it is shining rays of beauty and healing upon everyone! Love is one of the most powerful forces in the world. It is like having a golden ticket and everyone wants that ticket! Some people want that tremendous love that might have been elusive their whole life. Everyone wants to feel important and loveable. These are essential needs in life. If you don't have them, it can affect everything you do, say and feel. The world can sometimes feel cold. So, connect with your own heart first and bring the warm flame forth!

Action Plan:

1. **Be aware of what you might not accept about yourself**
2. **Be aware of what you might not accept about others**
3. **Say to yourself, "I am ok right now the way I am. I am improving every day to be more heartful, accepting and full of love for myself and others"**
4. **Opening my heart to myself can help me be more loving to others**

SUCCESS SAYING - " I love myself now. I don't have to be perfect."

BRILLIANT U TIP #16
LOVE YOUR OWN COMPANY

Goal: Being 100% Ok On Your Own

Being an independent individual means that you are self-sufficient. You know how to feed your own self-esteem, be your own cheerleader, comfort, protect and support yourself. The awesome part of being independent is that you are in control of yourself and no one is having to control you. If someone says something nice to you, you can say "thank you" and go upon your merry way. If someone says something nasty or unkind, you can take a minute to process and see if there is any information to be learned from that negative interaction. Is there anything that fits where you can take personal responsibility for your behavior? If not, then you can say to them, "that is unkind and doesn't hold any truth." You can also say to yourself, "I will not let what they said affect how I think or feel about myself."

Loving your own company and being ok alone is a must. When you are an adult, not needing another person in order to be ok is so important. You are just great on your own! You can figure things out. You can find work, support yourself, and take care of yourself! Being alone is not the same as being lonely. Being totally happy on your own is what a lot of people want and don't always know how to achieve. They will want what you have. You can learn how to shower yourself with good things and not wait for others to do it for you or with you. Others may not know what you like exactly. It can be very beneficial to celebrate yourself in the way that you only know how you want to be celebrated. The point is learning how to bring the party vibe into your life and not waiting for someone else to bring it!

Ideas:

- **Buy yourself something nice (in moderation)**
- **Take yourself out to eat**
- **Pamper Time! Give yourself a manicure – pedicure – facial**
- **Shower yourself with recognition and acknowledgement**
- **For your birthday decorate the house to spice up your day**
- **Put on dance music that makes you feel like a million bucks**
- **Always be your #1 fan**
- **Always be your own cheerleader**

Action Plan:

1. **What do you "wait for others" to do for you or with you?**
2. **Assess any need for approval or recognition from others**
3. **Become aware of the need for permission from others in order for you to do what you want to do**

4. **Celebrate you**
5. **Give yourself the best (within reason)**
6. **Give yourself what you need in order to be happy**

SUCCESS SAYING - " I do what I want to do! My value is not dependent on others. I love me and my own company."

BRILLIANT U TIP #17

SURROUND YOURSELF WITH POWER SYMBOLS

Goal: Be Motivated

Learn how to motivate yourself. You know yourself better than anyone. What are you excited about? What do you love? What are your interests and/or passions? That is the source of your go-getter energy. It all lies in knowing what gets you up and going. Everyone is unique in what interests or motivates them. By surrounding yourself with power symbols you can bring in more feelings of empowerment and moxie. Moxie is something you can't buy. It is that full of life feeling. It's that courageousness, swagger and total assurance in yourself that so many people want! A person full of moxie goes after what they want without a second thought. And they believe that they will get it because they have worked extremely hard to become so incredibly good at what they do. That confidence is made over time and it feels fabulous to have permanently.

Decorate or carry items with you that bring energetic vibes, comfort, peace, beauty and moxie into your life!

What do you love?
Decorate your environment with:

- **Bright colored wall hangings, art, glitter, sparkles**
- **Colorful or classy furniture**
- **Power symbols (big glass diamonds, crosses, suns)**
- **Power animals (tigers, lions, eagles, etc)**
- **Pictures of you/ others in motion**
- **Inspirational quotes/sayings/pictures**

What makes you feel good?
Try these activities:

- **Play upbeat music**
- **Watch an empowering movie**
- **Spontaneously dance**
- **Sing when you feel like it**
- **Make a space for doing music, art, or a hobby**
- **Give back to the community - Become a volunteer at a homeless shelter**
- **Start a sport or join a group with similar interests**

Action Plan:

1. **Make a list. What do you love and what excites you?**
2. **Take responsibility for creating your own joy**
3. **Cut out pictures or decorate your environment with power objects**
4. **Start doing what ignites your fire of joy and exuberance--- it is infectious!**

SUCCESS SAYING - "I can inspire and motivate myself. I am fired up!"

UTILIZE EFFECTIVE COPING BEHAVIORS WHEN STRESSED

Goal: Healthy Decision Making

Stress is an unavoidable and real part of life. Too much stress can be seriously damaging to our minds, bodies, and emotions. It is then critical for daily practices for calming, relaxing and comforting the psyche and body in order to minimize the effects and get back to a state of equilibrium. I can't say it enough: self-care, self-care, self-care!

Suggestions for coping with stress or helping our emotional state can be as simple as a 20-minute rest to make us feel balanced and more at peace. It can be CBD oil from a reputable company. It can be pampering, or a walk in the forest, or time at the beach watching the waves crash against the rocks. There is so much beauty all around us for the experiencing. We have to find joy in the little things.

Sometimes reducing stress takes removing yourself from a situation and getting quiet time. Overstimulation is a real thing. The body can only take so much before it starts to shut down. Sometimes stress can be exacerbated by medical issues. So, it's a good idea to see your general doctor if you are experiencing any issues that are of concern for you.

Healthy coping behaviors are:

- **Stepping away from the cause of stress or distress**
- **Establishing a mantra: "It's going to be OK"**
- **Breathing slow and deep**
- **Going walking or run**
- **Going into nature**
- **Doing something fun!**
- **Getting off the computer or smartphone.**
- **Reading a book/**
- **Drinking hot tea**
- **Taking a hot shower**
- **Pampering the body**
- **Applying cold pack to your head or over your eyes**
- **Sitting in the sun for 20 minutes**
- **Sitting by the ocean, lake, stream or river and listening to the sounds of it flowing**
- **Be thankful daily**

Action Plan:

1. **Identify when you have had too much stress and need a break**
2. **Take a moment for yourself to rest or practice self-care**
3. **Do stress relieving activities**
4. **Find beauty in everyday life**
5. **Take moments throughout the day to be grateful**

SUCCESS SAYING -"I can soothe myself in times of stress or anxiety."

ENJOY YOUR BEAUTIFUL LIFE

Goal: Being Versus Doing

There is value in taking the time to slow down and not be so busy all the time. There needs to be time to enjoy this beautiful life. Sometimes doing too much can have adverse effects. A balanced life is ideal. You have to ask yourself if you are working too much. Loving the journey is as important as getting to the finish line. Remember, thoughts have life and if you think of the reasons why you have a beautiful life, then you will. If you look for the golden nuggets all around us, you will find them. What you look for, what you focus on, is what you will get more of! Start looking for what to celebrate. Congratulate yourself for the accomplishments you have made! Look for what is beautiful about your life. Avoid comparing your life to another's. The truth is, rarely is someone's life as idyllic as you perceive it as being.

To put an end to the negative spiral of wishing you were somewhere else, doing something else, it takes deep appreciation for what you have in this moment. It also takes getting excited about all the things that you are doing and what you want to do in this life. In whatever form it takes. Even if it is minor; you are doing it! Happiness is not over there anymore. It is here, now! It is in your hands and you can relax into the beauty of knowing and living that reality!

Happiness is a state of mind. Happiness is created on the inside and projected outward. Be a magnet for all good things. Raise your vibration to a high level one and people will love to be around you. You will become a great source of warmth and comfort for others. The secret to happiness is not what you have in material wealth. Some of the wealthiest people in the world are some of the unhappiest people. This book has given you many priceless keys to unlock the treasures of your own ability to manufacture your own sunshine and happiness! Here you go onward and upward to greater things!

Action Plan:

1. **Slow down and take a moment to close your eyes and breathe!**
2. **Start looking for the beauty that is all around you**
3. **Start enjoying the journey and stop focusing only on getting to the destination**
4. **Have the courage to do what you really want to do**
5. **Create joy and exciting experiences**
6. **Count your blessings again and again**

SUCCESS SAYING - "Thank you for all my blessings and for what I have. I am filled with love, light and goodness. I am kind and I attract all good things into my life. I am happy. I am healthy. I am led to answers to any difficult situation I am facing. I have abundance in my life."

My Story:

I was born into a family with many extremely talented, successful and legendary relatives. Hard work and ambition were in the blood. One relative, whom I have a lot in common with, my grandmother's cousin Rudi Gernreich, was a Famous Fashion Designer who designed the thong underwear and topless bathing suit. He was also a dancer. My great grandfather was Karl Kautsky, who is known for being a Marxist Theorist and leader of the German Social Democratic Party.

My grandmother, mother, father, brother and myself were and are all artists. My father was also a multi-talented singer and musician. My Grandfather was a gastrointestinal surgeon based in Hawaii. This is relevant because over-achieving has been a way of life from an early age. Self-care and taking care of the family emotionally was way down on the list of priorities. The lack of value placed on nurturing the emotions affected me for many years.

Because of my mother's dissatisfaction with the status quo, she broke from the norm and went on a quest of psychological exploration and spirituality. That choice was bittersweet, yet in the end became a tremendous treasure for our family.

My path was that of constant achievement while suffering incredibly on the inside emotionally. The negative experiences of abandonment, emotional neglect, emotional/physical/sexual/mental abuse changed my once sunny confident disposition to one of doubt, insecurity, and depression.

My first memories of wanting to escape from my painful reality started at 5 years of age, when I wanted to run away. At 8 years old, I began the use of substances with smoking a cigarette every once and a while. At 12, it advanced to occasionally using harder substances and drinking to escape the pain. At 16, I developed Anorexia and suffered with that on and off for the next several years.

In high school, my journey for seeking deeper meaning and true comfort commenced. I lost interest in the social scene, as it was not satisfying for me as it once was. I had achieved things I had always wanted and yet the accomplishments did not make me happy as I thought they would. Since I could not find happiness in the outside world, I went inside myself to find it. I chose to spend my time listening to my most favorite music and taking hour long walks. Enigma was one of my favorite albums and it helped me connect with my emotions. These beautiful emotions were what I had always needed and wanted. I needed positive experiences to balance out the negative ones of my past. I felt fabulous at times and so connected to myself I thought I had made it. Yet, it was like a cracked golden chalice. The good feelings dwindled away and I was then left in the depression. This only showed me that the work was not done yet and I had to keep going.

I thought my love life would be the answer to everything wrong in my life. It would right all the wrongs and the hurts and heal me! Since we attract ourselves, I attracted a damaged person to me. My first major boyfriend turned out to be physically violent towards me, which almost cost me my life. Leaving him changed my life forever in a beneficial way.

A powerful passion took hold of my life, where I wanted to learn everything I could about healing and change through self-help books, counseling, holistic health, and higher education where I earned a Master's Degree in Marriage and Family Therapy. The more I learned, the better my life became due to making healthier choices. The more I learned about emotional independence and re-parenting the self, the more I was able to put myself first. I started protecting and taking care of myself holistically. I protected my precious energy and made better decisions about who I allowed in my life and close to me. If they hurt me, I put distance between us or ended the relationship or interaction entirely. Making that crucial decision made me feel 100% safe and increased my personal happiness. Feeling safe gave birth to new thoughts and emotions of everything being ok, and my symptoms dissipated. I no longer needed alcohol, drugs, shopping, and relationships to help me feel good temporarily. I started to feel better and better for longer and longer stretches.

I have achieved many things in my life that I had always wanted. And I will continue to go after and achieve more things that I have always wanted to. Having the courage to try and the willingness to fail is actually a great way of approaching one's life. I built my courage every day! I had to bring it back to life and harness it!

Allowing God into my life and giving Him total credit for everything has also been a huge part of feeling at peace in my life. God brought my husband to me and that opened the door to many great blessings in my life. God Blessed us with a beautiful, healthy and incredibly smart daughter that we are both grateful for.

My story is one to show others that making long lasting positive changes, healing and reclaiming the heart and sunshine self is possible! I am living proof! I did it! You can too! I cleared out the old, dead parts of my life that were no longer serving me, held and healed the injured parts and was ultimately victorious. The abusers could never keep my fierce spirit down forever, even though they tried! The fire breaks through and becomes a force to be reckoned with. It is a beautiful thing to watch in oneself and others!

By reading this book, you will find all the suggestions and support you need for the reclamation process you are striving for. When you really want it you will feel the fire burning so bright that the journey of self-improvement and bringing your spirit fully back to life will happen!

Best to you in your journey! I am cheering you on all the way!

Printed in the United States
by Baker & Taylor Publisher Services